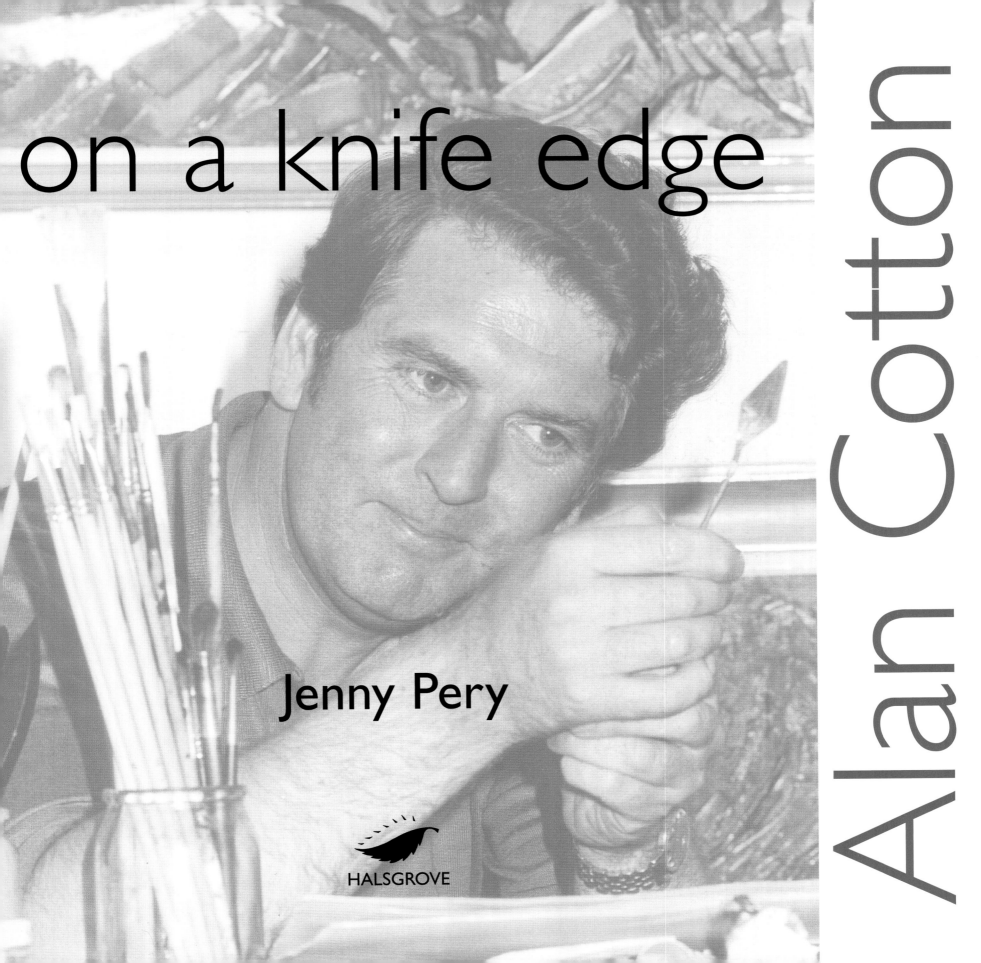

on a knife edge

Alan Cotton

Jenny Pery

HALSGROVE

First published in 2003 by Halsgrove
© 2003 David Messum Fine Art Limited
text © 2003 Jenny Pery

ISBN 1 84114 319 7

British Library Cataloguing-in-Publication-Data
A CIP data record for this book is available from the British Library

HALSGROVE
Halsgrove House
Lower Moor Way
Tiverton EX16 6SS
T: 01884 243242
F: 01884 243325
www.halsgrove.com

Printed and bound in Italy
by D'Auria Industrie Grafiche Spa

Designed by
The Studio Fine Art Publications

Studio Publications is part of
David Messum Fine Art Ltd

Dedication

I have been fortunate to have had two very special women in my life – my wife and best friend, Pat, with whom I have shared so many amazing experiences and my mother, Elsie, who against all odds, enabled me to go to art college to study painting and set me off on my career.

To my children, Juliette, Robin, Richard and Rachel, who have been a constant joy, enriching my life, together with their partners and their delightful and ever increasing 'off spring'.

To Norman Neasom, my friend, tutor and mentor, who, when I was a student, taught me how to draw during our cycling trips through the Worcestershire countryside.

To David and Millie Messum, Carol Tee and Michael Child, from the gallery, for their friendship and support during our adventurous years together.

To Jenny Pery for her patience and sensitive interpretation in the writing of this book.

To Michael Beddoe, good friend and master framer, whose splendid frames have enhanced my paintings through many exhibitions, and to my photographer John Saunders, for his ability to portray the rich impasto elements of my work in print.

Alan Cotton

MARCH 2002. Alan Cotton is in his studio beginning a new period of painting. His imagination has been fired by a recent trip to Morocco and he is poring over a sheaf of drawings to select elements for his paintings. The area around Marrakech, where the High Atlas mountains shimmer in the distance, has filled his mind with completely new sensations of colour. The whole ambience of that magical place, especially in the brilliant evening light, has generated more new ideas than he can ever hope to get into his paintings. But he cannot wait to make a start. 'When something thrills me there's an urgency about getting it down. It's the evening light that really turns me on. When I'm out prospecting I'm in and out of the car so much, driving along, screeching to a halt, it's that kind of excitement. I do a lot of walking too, walking very fast, to find special places. Without the constant renewal of images and ideas and the excitement of finding those special places, I don't think I would paint.'

Alan's ambitions for his Moroccan series are high, and he also feels the pressure of other people's expectations. Back at home in his studio he

Alan Cotton on a knife edge

immediately begins work on a very large canvas. After three days he has realised that he is not getting the results he wanted. The new colour combinations he has seen in Morocco contained a vibrancy and luminosity that he is finding impossible to reproduce with opaque pigment. The very different imagery is forcing him to rethink his painting methods, to invent, to discover new ways of mark-making. He needs to take a step back and spend time considering his next move. This temporary hiatus is nerve-racking but in itself exciting. New painting grounds are forcing new discoveries in paint.

Without this renewed sense of adventure the activity of painting can become routine and the work jaded. To Alan Cotton these trips abroad have become increasingly important as a means of refreshing his vision. He needs to reclaim that old excitement in front of the landscape, the excitement that first turned him into a painter. 'I remember as a child sitting down and seeing barley heads against a blue sky and thinking that was the most lyrical and marvellous thing you could see.' For the young Alan the landscape was full of romance. Equally delightful was the creamy, juicy texture of oil paint. His childhood passions for the countryside and for paint are now synthesised in his paintings, which are paraphrases in which he attempts with paint to produce an equivalent to the scene represented. Finding the telling paraphrase is often difficult. "People have a romantic idea about painting, they often think the work does itself, but it isn't like that at all. They don't understand the struggle you have – that's not a complaint, it's just the reality of the work. There are days when it's really hard – but there are other days when it's so joyous, it's almost as if your hand's being guided." [1]

Venice – Parallel Reflections
Canvas 24 × 24 ins

Olive Orchard, after the Storm *(detail)*

Provence – Olive Orchard, after the Storm
Oil on canvas 20 x 24 ins

WHEN ALAN COTTON picks a new painting ground, he prefers to get to know as much about it as possible, its history, and the way the inhabitants live. He is not interested so much in the topography as in what determines the contours and the manmade elements of the land. "In my view, no artist, no matter how talented, can just turn up at a place for the first time, out of the blue, and casually produce a convincing, lasting statement about it. You must get to know your scene; you must understand something of the people, the history, and the pace of life to allow the landscape to find its way under your skin." [2] Alan requires each of his paintings to build into itself all the sights and sounds and tastes and smells of the land, becoming as far as possible a visual equivalent to all the sensations he experienced there.

For the last twenty years Alan Cotton has been painting full-time. His output is as prodigious as his energy. He paints in his studio every morning, often from the early hours, and is a firm believer in Matisse's maxim 'never a day without a line'. In the studio he works fast, with complete concentration, while the sound of his favourite

never a day without a line

operas fill the air. Each painting trip yields sketchbooks full of drawings, and it is these drawings that are the seed corn for paintings made in the studio. Confining himself to drawing 'on location' enables him to travel light. When, as a student, he loaded himself down with all the paraphernalia for oil painting in front of the motif, he found that it impeded his seeing, his primary experience. 'It is the mind which is the important thing, you need to have it uncluttered'. Back at home in the studio the process of invention begins. He stains his primed canvases to give himself a halftone to work on, usually with yellow ochre which he finds an 'optimistic' colour. Onto this ground he draws with brushes in dilute madder brown or Prussian blue paint, composing his subject carefully. As he says, 'whereas much of painting is very intuitive, composition is a very sophisticated business. Very often you start with an abstract, structural, idea for the painting in your head. You take the rectangle which defines the painting you are embarking on and within that rectangle you start placing elements, thinking not of the buildings or trees that might make up the picture but of the abstract shapes underlying them. Essentially you are constructing an abstract design from little blocks of shapes, adding, subtracting and altering these shapes to create interesting relationships. It's important to take your thinking away from the original landscape idea for a time to allow you to construct a satisfying balance of shapes.'

Having invented a satisfactory composition by blending elements from his sketchbooks with remembered images and ideas, Alan builds colour on to his canvas. He uses a selection of painting knives, finding them capable of making an infinite variety of marks. He rarely uses the flatter palette knives, even for mixing large masses of paint on his palette, preferring the range and flexibility of the trowel-shaped

painting knives. His favourite five or six knives can cope with both delicate delineation and broad slabs of paint, and he handles them with a skill acquired through long experience. He is often questioned about the slabby nature of the paint and the jutting edges thrown up by the knife. On one occasion during a talk a member of the audience asked what he was going to do about these 'ragged bits' of paint. 'Why, do you have a problem with them?' enquired Alan. 'No, no problem, I would simply take out my scissors and cut them all off' was the reply. Alan's studio is well supplied with paint. He loves having great stacks of paint around him, in tubes waiting to be started or in piles on his palette. 'When I was a kid I was deprived of paint. Now I love having an abundance of things – lots of paint, lots of canvases. I love to have enough so that I can afford to spoil a few. With only one or two canvases there's too much at stake.' His paint store covers a very wide range of colours, as he works in many different colour keys. He uses colour intuitively, letting it follow its own logic, working from dark to light, partly in deference to traditional practice, and partly because the lighter colours – titanium white or flake white mixed with a little

the painting knife is infinitely versatile

naples yellow – are such lovely colours to put on. 'It's a delight, like eating a cream cake. It's best to work up to the experience of the big bite at the end'.

Nowadays Alan uses only painting knives to apply the paint, finding that they can rapidly provide the lush impasto that he loves. 'The painting knife is infinitely versatile in the number of marks it can produce, depending on the amount of paint you pick up, the angle of the blade, the pressure you apply... The richness of surface with the textures and the kind of mark I use are the very essence of my work.' [3] He admits, though, that the knife does create some problems, using much more paint than a brush, which can make the drying time much longer, often taking up to eight months for a large canvas to dry. The resulting surface quality of the painting is both more chopped up in the worked areas and glassier in the broad areas of paint. With a knife the paint cannot readily be messed around on the canvas but needs bold, decisive placing.

The metaphor of the 'knife edge' dramatically illustrates the struggle going on in the studio. Painting can be something of a tightrope walk, especially when a picture refuses to work. 'Painting is a much more complex schema than drawing. Through using colour and texture you can give an emotional experience that a drawing can't do. You are trying to use all the ingredients at your disposal – great chunks of impasto or staining and scraping back to the canvas, as in the Moroccan paintings. Marks are important. Each mark is a record of physical action. When a child spills his food and puts his fingers through it, you can see the traces of the mark. You can read a Van Gogh painting by the eloquence of the mark. Impressionist painting attracts people without their realising it because of the spontaneity of the mark... If you are a painter, you look beneath the surface of a painting to find out about the experience the artist is trying to give you.'

A LAN COTTON'S DESIRE to paint seems to have been conceived early, although there was no hint of any artistic ability in his family. He was born in Redditch in 1938, the third of four children, a girl followed by three boys. The family of six lived in a very small two-up two-down terraced house on the edge of town. Because the front room was always kept tidy for special occasions, the family were mostly confined to one room downstairs. The war and post-war years in the Midlands were difficult. Alan's father, William Cotton, had left school at the age of twelve to become a plough driver. As an agricultural labourer and factory worker, he was all too conscious of his lowly place in the prevailing social order. He was often out of work, and when he could get it, work was a mind-numbing business. For him real life began at the pub in the evening. Between games of dominoes he joined his neighbours in drinking and giving vent to a widespread sense of oppression.

Alan's mother, Elsie May Annie Dingley, came from a rather different background. The Dingleys had at one time been a wealthy Worcestershire family,

anything to earn a bob or two

and Elsie's father was a carpenter and wheelwright. Elsie herself had received little education, and she married the boy next door. She had no aspirations for herself other than to make a living and ensure the survival of her family. Money was always a problem, and Alan remembers hiding when the rent man came around. He regards the sentimentally invoked 'working class unity' as a myth, and remembers only each individual's struggle for survival. Drinking in the pub was the great opiate. Friday was payday, and by the time the men arrived home via the pub the housekeeping money was always reduced. It was Alan's mother who coped with the household's financial problems, and she worked all hours of the day to help make ends meet. She left the house at 6.30 am to clean offices and was back home at 8.30 to get the children off to school. From midday until 3pm she worked as a school dinner supervisor, and then cleaned more offices in the evening. She also took in washing. Her remarkable physical energy and her stoicism through her long working days set an example that Alan has never forgotten.

William Cotton often involved his children in doing jobs for neighbours. Even within the prevailing culture of 'anything to earn a bob or two' it was embarrassing to be so readily volunteered by a father to do labouring jobs for others. Nobody could afford to pay a coalman to deliver coal, but the Cotton boys would do it for a shilling. They were made to queue for pieces of coke at the gasworks two miles away and deliver the bags of coke for the neighbours by bicycle or sledge. When his father returned home from the pub, he would extract money from Elsie's housekeeping budget and send his boys out to buy extra beer for him. Alan resented this almost nightly ritual and it became a competition

Pat and Alan Cotton with Elsie Cotton
(Alan's mother) 1977 *(opposite)*

Bill and Elsie Cotton, 1959 *(below)*

amongst the boys either to avoid it or to see how quickly they could get it done. Alan used to run the mile each way from Albert Street to The Crown with an old cider bottle to collect the beer. One disastrous night he dropped the bottle on the way home, sending both beer and money down the drain.

From early childhood Alan was industrious. He did a morning newspaper round, worked on a milk float, and ran all sorts of errands, usually arriving late for school. At the age of sixteen he was working in a butcher's shop four evenings a week and on Saturday mornings. He was not particularly big or strong for his age and found the work – carrying huge sides of beef in and out of the shop and pushing old bones in bags through the town on a bicycle – both hard and humiliating.

In his spare time, from a very early age, Alan painted. It is painting, not drawing, that he remembers. To keep him occupied when he was very small, his mother made paintbrushes for him out of her own hair, tied onto a stick with cotton. These served well with liquid poster paint, but he was later given hard tablets of paint and can still remember scrubbing at these to extract the colours. When he was nine he belonged to a club which brought a man to the house every Friday evening selling various items for a fixed weekly sum. Alan acquired a set of watercolour paints of indifferent quality but with a wide range of colours. The splendid array of colours contrasted excitingly with the post-war urban dinginess. Just looking at these colours spurred him on to use them. He would escape from the town into the surrounding countryside as often as he could to paint in the fields.

Painting took him out of the monochrome grime of the town into a landscape where the light sparkled on ears of corn, where the colours were fresh, and where he could create his own perfect world, a pastoral idyll like that of a Samuel Palmer painting. The landscape became the stuff of his dreams, and painting it became a romantic escape from the realities of home life. Most of his early painting was done out in the countryside, but after the family moved to his grandfather's house in a better area of town, he did some painting at home – large pictures of cricketers and sportsmen or film stars, using oil paint on canvas or paper laid on the floor. He still remembers his Aunt Gladys objecting to the heaps of canvases stacked around the house. At his primary school Alan was criticised by the teachers for spending too much time painting, and was caned on the hand for drawing in class. However, he can still remember the jars of paint that the school provided and the romance of the colour 'leaf green'.

In his neighbourhood Alan was the oddity – the kid from primary school who passed his 11+ and went to Grammar School. Amongst his siblings he was the only Grammar School kid, although his younger brother Bernard went to Oxford and later to London University to do his doctorate. Bernard was appointed the first Professor of Furniture History in Britain. His elder brother Alfred, working in industry, became an important union official for the AEU. His sister Dorothy emigrated to Australia, where she sadly died. The Grammar School added to the

family's money worries – how could they afford Alan's uniform? His mother was ambitious for Alan and somehow she managed it. She even persuaded her husband to give the sixteen-year-old Alan pocket money of ten shillings a week, and kept him to it despite the ensuing arguments.

In Redditch the boys grew up rough. There was gang warfare among the children. Alan belonged to the Albert Street gang, and was several times cornered by rival gangs. On one occasion he and his brother were surrounded and had stones thrown at them. Alan threw a retaliatory stone which broke a boy's glasses and cut his eye. For several days afterwards he was afraid to go to school in case this got him into trouble. His family's poor circumstances caused him other difficulties. There was no room at home to do homework. Alan became something of a renegade at school and was very nearly expelled. Out of school, also, he was always getting into trouble. One snowy winter a sledge sliced through his leg during a toboggan race. For Guy Fawkes day his gang prepared a bonfire in their street with a quantity of tarred roofing felt mixed in with the wood. A rival gang lit the Albert Street bonfire a few days too soon, and Alan, trying to put it out, got some burning roofing felt wrapped around his leg. His screams of pain brought his mother and the neighbours running from their houses. They had real difficulty getting rid of the burning tar and dressing the extensive burns.

At the Grammar School Alan was the kid who was good at Art, and he was asked to make all the posters. In the art exams, however, he always came second, never first, as first place seemed to be reserved for the son of the art teacher, Rodney Hodge. When Mr Hodge left he was replaced by Ted Holmes, a young teacher from the Lake District who took Alan under his wing. Ted Holmes became Alan's first role model of a working artist. 'He seemed very much the romantic artist to me. He was tall and gaunt, wore sandals and had very long hair. And he had been to Lancaster School of Art and drew very well. He seemed to take to me. So much so that I used to spend time at his house with him, and I also went up to the Lake District where he let me have his studio for part of the summer... He was a character who loved the visual arts, and who gave me the sense that the art world was a very rich way of life.' [4]

Out of school Alan spent hours looking at the paintings in Birmingham Art Gallery. He still remembers the impact that B. W. Leader's *February Filldyke* and Stanhope Forbes' *Village Philharmonic* had on him. It was also in Birmingham Art Gallery, as part of a loan exhibition, that he saw his first Van Gogh painting and was amazed by the abundance and physicality of the paint. He stood in front of the painting and thought 'that is what I want to do'. Van Gogh has always inspired him although later in life he was also particularly influenced by Soutine and Nicholas de Stael. Amongst British artists he was drawn to the romantic landscapes of Alan Reynolds and the knife paintings of Kyffin Williams.

Rodney Hodge had left Redditch County High School to become Principal of Redditch School of Art. Needing to keep up his quota of students in order to

'Elsie Cotton' drawn by Alan, aged 17 years

Drawing of 'Tree Stump' (and below) while a student at Redditch School of Art, 1956

qualify for diploma status, he persuaded Alan to enlist at Redditch School of Art. Alan's O-levels had not gone well, having been disrupted by an attack of peritonitis from which he nearly died, and so, at the age of seventeen, he joined the school. Redditch School of Art was tiny, with only eight full-time students. To Alan, Rodney Hodge seemed a frustrated painter who had never realised his ambitions and who was disparaging to others with artistic pretensions, maintaining that it was impossible to make a living as an artist without teaching. He and Alan never understood each other. Alan used to wear a lumberjack's hat with dewlaps to which he was so firmly attached that he never took it off, even in class. This hat infuriated Mr Hodge. Alan, in his turn, was alienated by Mr Hodge's teaching methods. His 'teaching' usually consisted of pinning up, on a Monday morning, a reproduction of a painting by an artist such as Joan Miró or Max Ernst or Paul Klee and announcing that everyone must work in that artist's manner all week. No attempt was made to explain that the distinctive style of the work of art shown was the result of lengthy thought processes. The students were left floundering.

Alan's main interest was always in the landscape – his private perfectable world – and he stopped going into the Art School, preferring to work outside. It was from one of the other teachers, Norman Neasom, brought to Redditch from the big city, that Alan received most of his art education. Neasom treated Alan like a surrogate son and together they cycled all round the countryside, exploring a wide variety of subjects ranging from ecclesiastical stained glass to how to eat shellfish. Norman Neasom drew, and still draws, 'like an angel'. Working alongside him, Alan began to draw in a very natural way, using drawing as a thinking process in which a subject could be fully analysed prior to painting. Neasom taught Alan the importance of drawing informatively for painting. He

had an apt pupil. He later said of Alan 'I was immediately impressed by his outdoor sketchbook work. I knew from the start that there was great potential there.' [5] For Alan, Norman Neasom opened a whole world. 'Working alongside someone who draws brilliantly is a great education.'

Alan's continued absence from the art school studios finally brought about a visit from the inspectors. Alan had hired the offices of an old weighbridge down by the canal at Tardebigge to use as a studio, but had never shown the drawings that he had done there to Mr Hodge. It was Norman Neasom who warned Alan that the inspectors were coming the next day to interview him, and who suggested that he bring in his canalside drawings. Together they covered the walls of the art school with his large drawings of tree roots and of light and shade on the water. When the two inspectors, Mr Pickering and Mr Doubleday, demanded to see Alan's class work, he had little of any value to show them. They then looked at the drawings on the walls and asked whose they were. When Alan said they were his, Mr Hodge was utterly disbelieving, accusing him of lying. When he asked why Alan had never shown them to him, Alan replied 'because I can't talk to you'. Mr Pickering and Mr Doubleday, however, were impressed. They took Alan aside and told him that he was a real painter, that he was wasting his time in Redditch, and that he should leave. Within a week he had left.

Ruskin Hall, Bourneville School of Art, where Alan studied for a year, was a stepping stone for entry into Birmingham College of Art. It provided an excellent and enjoyable foundation course, in which students studied a range of subjects such as architecture and anatomy. Despite this good foundation, however, Alan felt like an outsider at Birmingham College of Art. Throughout his three years there he lived at home and travelled the fourteen miles into Birmingham by bus every day. He had already had some success exhibiting and selling work at the Royal Birmingham Society of Artists, but he never mentioned this in college, where he sensed that commercial success was frowned upon. Many of the tutors were frustrated artists who could not offer advice to their students on how to

make a living as a painter. They resented having to teach, however, preferring either to get on with their own work or socialise in the pub at lunchtime. To Alan, the general level of tuition seemed pretty dismal and their explanations and advice obscure. For him the principal, Gilbert Mason, was no exception. 'One day in the reverential hush of the life class I was aware of a presence behind me, of a smoker whose smoke was coming over my shoulder. It seemed like an eternity that he stood behind me without saying a word. Suddenly he elbowed me aside and picked up a rag, got some paint off the palette and started to rub bits out. Satisfied, he threw down the rag and said 'that's bloody better, boy' and walked off. That was the level of criticism.'

Alan knew that teaching could be better than this. He had a natural ability to teach, having learnt from Ted Holmes and Norman Neasom the importance of putting oneself on the same level as the student in order to understand his point of view, and then give straightforward, sensible advice. It was a natural progression for Alan to do a postgraduate teacher training year at Birmingham University. University gave him the tools of analytical thought, turning him into a skilled communicator. Both Grammar School and six years of art education had brought him a long way from his background, where words were sparingly used. His father was not an articulate man, relying largely on the basic exchange of clichés acceptable at the pub. William Cotton was always trying to persuade his sons to accompany him to the pub. Alan usually resisted. Pub talk was

Drawing of his first studio in June 1956 at Tardebigge, Worcestershire, at a farm once owned by poet A.E. Houseman's brother

completely alien to him, and seemed to him to conceal rather than reveal ideas. The newly discovered tools of mental analysis seemed an amazing gift that he could bring to bear on his own circumstances as well as on those of the art world. He became as interested in sociology as he was in art history.

Armed with the fruit of the tree of knowledge, he developed a buccaneering approach to life. He would take on any teaching or lecturing that was available, partly for the fun of it and partly for the ever-present necessity to earn a few shillings. This attitude landed him in some uncharted waters, in which he, like Lucky Jim, was often out of his depth. On one occasion he was engaged by the Workers Education Authority to lecture on Michelangelo and the Italian Renaissance to a group of rather grand people in a distant village. He arrived in his very old car, nicknamed Petroleum Blownapart, to be met by people with intimidatingly posh accents who invited him to leave his car and be escorted by them to the big house for drinks after the lecture. This unfamiliar social procedure rapidly degenerated into the stuff of nightmare as Alan emerged from the big house to find the village swathed in a thick blanket of fog. Searching for his car in the fog, he climbed over a fence to be met by barking dogs and an irate man in pyjamas loudly berating him: 'You're the bloody idiot who blocked my drive!'. When Alan was finally permitted to get into his dripping car the engine refused to start and the old man was forced to push the car out of his drive and all the way down the village street. The vision of the old gent in pyjamas pushing Petroleum Blownapart in the fog amuses Alan to this day.

Alan's teacher training at Birmingham University included a term's teaching practice at Bridley Moor Secondary School in Redditch. It was there that he met a young English and Drama teacher in her first term teaching in the school where she had been a pupil. Patricia Stanley immediately caught Alan's eye, and he wrote her name in the back of his sketchbook in order to remember it. He was too shy to ask her out until the very last day of term, when he plucked up enough courage to ask her for a drive in Petroleum Blownapart. They drove around with the rain coming through the roof between them. However, neither the rain nor Alan's previous engagement to another girl called Pat, impeded their romance. Years later, looking through his old sketchbooks, he found the name 'Patricia Stanley' portentously written there.

Pat was the unexpected daughter of a sixteen-year old girl, Freda, who had fallen for a businessman from Bolton, a married man with three children. As there was no state support available at that time, there was no question of Freda's being able to keep the child. One of Freda's sisters worked with a woman, Rose, who already had one daughter but was unable to have more children. With Rose she made an unofficial arrangement. When the baby Pat was ten days old she was put in a carrycot and handed over to her new mother. There were no adoption papers of any sort because Freda absolutely refused to sign away her baby. Rose never made any distinction between her two girls, and Pat was seventeen before she was told who her natural mother was and was able to meet her for the first time. After this it did not take her long to track down her natural father at work and announce 'I'm your daughter'. Father and daughter became firm friends. Freda later married and had two daughters with whom Pat still gets on famously.

Alan was attracted by Pat's womanly curves and naturally sunny nature. Pat admired Alan's good looks and also his formidable energy. Nothing seemed to daunt him, and Pat soon learned that whenever Alan mooted an idea, it was already well on its way to becoming reality. There was no doubt in Pat's mind that he was already a committed painter. He never went anywhere without a sketchbook, and it was clear to Pat that if he had come from an artistic background he would never have gone into teaching. But, at the time when they met, teaching seemed the only viable way of making a living. On obtaining his Dip Ed Alan answered an advertisement and found himself a multi-faceted job in the Forest of Dean – in charge of Art at Lydney Grammar School in the mornings,

Pen and ink drawings of Snowdonia, 1974 *(and below)*

Snowdonia, 1974 *Oil on canvas* 20 × 40ins

and teaching Painting in the afternoons and Art History in the evenings at Lydney Art School. When they got engaged Pat was still teaching in Redditch and living with her foster mother who kept a greengrocer's shop on the main road. Very early every Monday morning Alan would drive past on his way to work, while Pat waited at the window for him to appear so that she could rush downstairs in her dressing gown and snatch a kiss amongst the potatoes.

Pat on the day she and Alan became engaged, 1960

Alan and Pat at Bicton Park

WHEN THEY MARRIED in 1961 Pat found herself a teaching job at Coleford Secondary Modern School. The couple saved Pat's salary and raised a mortgage to buy their first home. This was Rocks Cottage in St Briavels, which consisted of two small cottages run together, and contained a bed left behind by the previous owner, one white chair, two stools and two orange boxes covered with a tablecloth. Together they worked on the house to make it habitable and at one end Alan built himself a studio. They both wanted children and the first two of their four children, Juliette and Robin, were born at St Briavels. Alan loved being a father, finding his relationship with his children, very different from that of his own parents, a source of immense pleasure. There was very little money, however, to support the growing family. Alan taught all day, on his afternoons off, and in the evenings and weekends to make ends meet. Despite these stringencies the couple never had a single argument about money. When she was first married Pat turned on the radio to listen to 'Friday Night is Music Night', just as she had listened to it as a child with her foster mother. 'Turn it off – I can't bear it' Alan

painting with the knife is the way to go

implored. 'When I was a child that programme was the background noise for rows about money.'

It was at St Briavels that Alan met John Berger. John Berger used to live in the Forest of Dean with the Dutch painter Friso ten Holt. The erotic paintings with which they adorned their house caused a sensation amongst the villagers. Berger had recently published his book *Permanent Red*, which had made a deep impression on Alan. Berger returned to St Briavels with the photographer Jean Mohr in order to work on his book *A Fortunate Man*, featuring the local doctor, John Eskell. Dr Eskell had looked after Pat when Juliette was born and, during his many visits to the house, had seen Alan's work and admired it. He asked if he could bring his friend John Berger to see the work. Full of trepidation, Alan agreed. One Sunday morning he was up late in his pyjamas emptying the ashes in the garden, when he saw Berger and the doctor making their way towards him over the horizon. He dashed indoors, threw on some clothes and opened up his studio. When Berger arrived he took time to look at all the work, and asked to see the student drawings as well. He particularly admired some drawings that Alan had made looking down from a rock face, asking how Alan had managed to do them. On the easel were Alan's first two paintings made with a knife. They were somewhat influenced by Nicholas de Stael and Kyffin Williams, using very simple strokes of the knife. Berger remarked 'You have a feel for paint. And I really think the knife is the way for you to go'. Although in those days Alan had hardly explored the potential of the knife and had little notion of the mark as a metaphor, it was clear that the malleability of oil paint excited him. For Alan this was a seminal meeting. John Berger confirmed his instinct about the direction his work should take. Alan has painted with a knife ever since that day.

His studio at St. Briavels in the Wye Valley 1964

Wye Valley – St. Briavels Common, Evening
Oil on canvas 20 × 30 ins

Wye Valley – Storm Clouds over St. Briavels
Oil on canvas 28 × 36 ins

Wye Valley – St. Briavels Common, Winter
Oil on canvas 36 × 48 ins

St Briavel's Common *was one of Alan's first knife paintings, only recently completed when John Berger visited him in his studio in the Forest of Dean. Its ingenuous directness and freshness reflect Alan's delight in the new circumstances of his life at that time and his excitement at finding new ways to express his happiness in paint. 'I was a very young guy, recently married, we had a small child, and we found ourselves in a new part of the country. Everything about our lives was fresh, and we seemed to be right on top of the world in St Briavel's, where our neighbours were simple farming people, and our outlook was all sky with great clouds passing across it. I was trying to make a statement about the freshness of our lives on that common. I hadn't used a painting knife very much, and it was a superb experience spreading those large simple masses of paint. The painting itself was as much an adventure as the newness of our life.'*

St Briavel's Common, 1965
Oil on board 36 × 48 ins

IN THE FOREST OF DEAN Alan worked hard to establish an economic base for his family. By now his son Robin had been born. Despite the hectic teaching days he found time to make his own paintings, which he exhibited in local Wye Valley exhibitions. He longed to have more time for painting and found working in school extremely time-consuming. 'Lecturing' at a higher level would give him more space, and in order to do so he needed more qualifications. It still did not seem possible to Alan to earn a living by painting. It was important to a man of his background to be a good provider for his family and to have a 'proper job'. Painting pictures was most definitely not a 'proper job'. The solution seemed to be to do a further degree. In 1966 he came south to Exeter University to do a year's Advanced Diploma of Education.

The year in Exeter gave Alan time to explore the intellectual side of art. He wrote a dissertation on Creative Thinking, drawing conclusions from his researches that have informed his own attitude to art ever since. His study of art in schools convinced him that the activity of drawing is for human beings both

painting pictures was not a proper job

natural and universal. When organising an exhibition of paintings by Japanese children he found the Japanese drawings to be almost the same as those of European children. All children, it seemed, instinctively use a certain common iconography and possess a natural talent that, at some stage during ageing, may be lost. It is Alan's belief that this natural talent should be preserved and cherished.

The whole family accompanied Alan to Devon for an idyllic year. They rented a delightful house in Topsham from the Deputy Vice Chancellor of Exeter University. Pat found herself a teaching job locally. When a job came up at the teacher training college, Rolle College in Exmouth, Alan gladly responded to an invitation to apply for it and beat off 120 other applicants to get it. He sold Rocks Cottage and rented a family house on a farm at Clyst St Mary.

Being Senior Lecturer in Art and Design at Rolle College did indeed give Alan more time for his own painting. College life also had its own rewards. He enjoyed exploring ideas in the company of like-minded people and found interaction with the students stimulating. He gave a great deal of his energy to teaching, running summer schools and weekend courses in the holidays. He also took a vigorous part in many local activities, lecturing to amateur art societies and judging their work. At first the family had no permanent abode. The money they managed to scrape together would not, at current Devon prices, buy them a house with room for a studio, so they looked around for something to convert.

In 1968 Alan saw an advertisement for the sale of an old farm site covered with semi-derelict buildings. He borrowed the money to buy it and knew exactly what he wanted to do with it, but had difficulty working out the cash flow to do

it. He enlisted the help of his students at Rolle College to pull down the old buildings, spending dangerous days tying pillars and beams to the back bumper of his car and pulling them down by driving away. There were demolition parties at which huge bonfires were made and masses of beer drunk. Gradually the site was cleared and plans for a house were drawn. According to the Land Commission Bill regulations a start had to be made on the foundations by the first of April that year in order not to be severely fined – a fine they could not possibly have afforded to pay. The Cottons could not afford to pay full building costs, but a local builder agreed to lay the foundations by the due date. When the builder reneged on his agreement at the last minute, Alan was left with only forty-eight hours to his deadline. He asked a surveyor friend who lived nearby for help. The surveyor, Eric McDowell, arrived in the pouring rain with all his apparatus. With only seven hours to expiry time he and Alan measured and marked out the building, and started to put down lines with lime. With less than one hour to go Alan suddenly realised that he had no witness to the fact that a start on the house

had been made, and that he needed to have the letter he had typed signed and witnessed by a local notable before the midnight deadline. Alan ran through the rain to the house of Burgess Attwood, his local councillor. Peering through his curtains, he saw him sitting by the fire in dressing gown and slippers drinking a cup of cocoa. He rang the doorbell and the door was opened a crack. Alan's evident desperation finally allayed his suspicions. Councillor Attwood put on his wellington boots and a mackintosh over his pyjamas and went down the road in the rain. Under an umbrella Alan ceremoniously took a spade and dug a section of a trench, while the councillor solemnly signed his letter.

Economic necessity decided Alan to build his own house, working at weekends. It was a nerve-racking time, because he had to borrow money to buy all the building materials, the sand and cement, drainpipes, window and door frames. He was able to get good free advice and on this advice he built walls, a staircase, and a drainage system, to very high standards. He still regards the 'tumbling bay' manhole that he built in the garden as a work of art. When the building inspector was due to make his drain inspection Alan came straight from Rolle College to meet him. He was asked to go down the hole and put in a bung. Then he was told 'Mr Cotton, the drains are fine. Please go down and take out the bung, but be careful because there will be a rush of water'. Still in his suit, Alan descended and started to remove the bung, at which point there was a loud explosion. The bung shot out into the main sewer and water flooded up the manhole, saturating him completely. Alan can still see in his mind's eye the great grin on the building inspector's face as he hung over him in the manhole.

Exactly a year after Alan had dug his first trench the family moved in. Only

Laying the foundations for Brockhill Studio, 1968

the living room and one bedroom were complete, but gradually they built the rest of the house around themselves, the two children becoming part of the building team. It was discovered that Robin, aged four, had created his own little building site in the garden of their rented farmhouse, secreting bits of drainage pipe, damp course and broken bricks back there every time he visited the site. For the whole of that year Alan did no painting. However, he enjoyed the experience of building his own house and studio. He liked working with his hands, and loved doing all the woodwork and laying the floorboards. It was a different but satisfying form of creation, making a home for his family. And once the family were settled in the new house, two other children, Richard and Rachel, were born.

After twelve years of teaching at Rolle College, Alan was desperate to do his own work every day and to be in charge of his own destiny. His extra-curricular activities were beginning to clash with his commitments as a lecturer. He began making art films for BBC South West. While he was still lecturing at Rolle College, the freelance film-maker Bernard Grimsey had made a 16mm feature film about his work. Alan wrote to Tom Salmon, the head of BBC South West, asking if some of this film might be suitable for television. Alan received a postcard from Tom Salmon inscribed 'Dear Alan, meet me in The Otter. Last to

arrive buys the drinks'. The result of this meeting was Alan's film *A Step or Two Away the Picture is Complete*, directed by Kevin Crooks.

Alan's work was also gaining a wider audience as a result of the travelling exhibition arranged with Professor Molwyn Merchant, who showed his own sculpture. A further offer of a major exhibition at the Canada Arts Gallery in British Columbia had been proposed. Alan needed the time to paint. One momentous day in 1982 he came home from work at lunchtime. Pat was home from school, and Alan insisted on taking her out to lunch, saying that he wanted to have a serious talk. Pat feared the worst, thinking that he was about to disclose a torrid affair, but instead Alan announced: 'Look, I've really had it with teaching, I just want to paint every day of my life. I know that you're also finding

Alan and Pat with their children, L to R: Juliette, Richard, Rachel and Robin, 1981

teaching a strain. If you want to stop, let's give up on the same day. We'll start a new life together as a painter and business partner.'

Pat agreed. Both she and Alan resigned from their full-time teaching jobs, although Pat continued to do supply teaching. The children were told what was going to happen, with no objections allowed. Despite Pat's absolute faith that Alan would succeed as a painter, the first few years were extremely difficult financially. There were family business meetings at which the likely earnings from future exhibitions were pre-allocated, each child putting in a claim for his or her next new pair of shoes. Alan and Pat formed a legal partnership, and Pat took over the paperwork, but the whole family lent a hand to the enterprise. The children were a part of the team, helping Pat to stretch and prepare all the canvases and to paint the frames.

Devon – Wild Oats
against a Stormy Sky
Oil on canvas 24 × 18 ins

Alan continued to run private painting courses in the village hall, an activity he had already started while he was at Rolle College. All the family helped with these, serving lunches and teas to the students. He also lectured locally and worked increasingly on films with the BBC, particularly with Spotlight South West. During the 1980s he made a number of art educational films: *Out of the Box, The Moving Line, For the Sake of a Lick of Paint, Journeys into Light* and *An Artist on Every Corner*. These covered both art history and practical painting. It was while making a film about the Newlyn School painters that he first met the influential art dealer David Messum. David Messum's admiration for the work of the Newlyn artists was well known, and his exhibitions of their work had caused a national revival of interest. Alan was in Cornwall with his film crew at an auction where a painting by Thomas Cooper Gotch was being sold. David Messum arrived late and bought the painting for what was then a record price for Newlyn work. The film crew later visited him in his Beaconsfield gallery to film the Private View of the exhibition in which the Gotch painting

I met a dealer who…

appeared. It turned out that Messum had seen and been impressed by Alan's paintings of the North Devon coastline around Hartland Point. He gave Alan a London exhibition and took him on as one of his artists, for the first few years paying him an annual salary set against sales of paintings. The Cotton's financial situation was considerably eased.

Alan's first exhibition at Messum's, in the St George Street Gallery, was a success, and paved the way for sixteen increasingly successful exhibitions of Alan's work. His shows are now eagerly awaited and most of the paintings sell either from the catalogue or during the first few days on exhibition. A review by Graham Hughes of the 1988 exhibition sums up the impression created by Alan's work. 'Colour is the overall impact... This is a distinguished, memorable show. What I will treasure specially is the aroma of lavender from the field in the picture... I am grateful to this radiant exhibition for bringing it to London.'[6]

Devon – Snow in the Otter Valley
Oil on canvas 24 x 30 ins

Hartland, bought by Plymouth City Museum and Art Gallery, *was the first of Alan's paintings to be bought by a public collection. Alan first visited Hartland on the North Devon coast in the mid seventies. He returned many times over the next ten years, getting to know the area intimately. He estimates that he has probably made over eighty paintings of Hartland.* 'When I came down the hill into Hartland Quay for the first time and looked along the coast, the sheer drama of it was mind-blowing. It was a stormy day and the energy of that great solid mass of water constantly hitting the coastline was impressive. I used to look at one part of the coastline that I particularly liked and try and note all the changes, to work through different seasons, at different times of day and in different qualities of light. When you like something so much you want to hold on to it and explore it in all its moods. I began to think of the paintings as a series, as Monet did. Those Hartland paintings had to be large, and the application of paint had to be as energetic as the movement of the water on the rocks. The whole dynamic of the knife helped, because I could stand in front of big canvases and use my muscles to attack them with paint, dragging great masses of pigment across four feet of canvas. Every painting I made of Hartland was an attempt to look at the relationship between the static land strata and the movement of water coming in, constantly trying to erode it.'

Hartland, 1977
Oil on canvas 48 × 60 ins

DAVID MESSUM has become not only Alan's dealer but also a firm friend. From the first he has been sympathetic to the development of the work, and has on occasions painted alongside Alan on location. He has a painter's eye and, without prescribing a direction for the work, he has been a useful critic. 'Certain observations have helped me a lot. I had made a lot of Provence paintings looking down from a high viewpoint. Many of them had a small strip of sky at the top. David asked whether I needed any sky at all. It was a good idea.'

Alan has shown his gratitude for David Messum's support. In the dark days of the recession when Messum's were forced to close, Alan had an exhibition coming up. David telephoned him to say that the bank had suddenly decided to foreclose on him and the gallery was to be stripped that day. There was nowhere to show Alan's work. Alan suggested that they should put on the exhibition at David Messum's home, Lordswood, in Marlow. David agreed, but only on condition that the whole thing was done properly, just as it would be arranged in a London gallery. The Cottons pledged all their free capital to underwrite the show. It was a gamble. At Lordswood the studios were cleared and Alan's pictures hung, a good catalogue was produced, and good food and wine ordered for the Private View, which was due to start at 10 am on Saturday morning. On Saturday the apprehension in the studios was tangible. Nobody had arrived by 10.45 and everyone became increasingly nervous. But gradually people came, and the work started to sell. By Sunday evening every single painting had been sold. The Cottons and the Messums, hugely encouraged, sat late in the office drinking whisky. David Messum later presented Alan with the long list of sold paintings with their accompanying red dots as a memento of the occasion.

Alan, freed from teaching, began to travel in search of subject matter. In the 1970s he had painted extensively in the Devon landscape. One exhibition at Exeter University showed nothing but paintings of cows in the Otter valley. At the Private View an old Professor approached Alan: 'A word in your ear, Cotton. Why do you only paint cows from behind?' 'Well' joked Alan 'I haven't leant how to paint their heads yet.' 'Do you realise how Freudian that is?' the Professor commented earnestly. Alan was of course fully aware of the Freudian implications. Most painting, whether intentionally or unintentionally, contains sexual innuendoes, and landscape imagery is full of it. Alan remembers a day spent painting the headland at Tintagel. 'I was with another painter and we talked endlessly about how it looked like a female body and how we were exploring the crevices. There is a sensuality in the sweeping curves which resembles the human body. The sexual analogies can't be denied.'

In reaction to the softness of South Devon and the Otter Valley, Alan found the rocky cliffs of Hartland on the North Devon coast a ruggedly inspiring subject. He spent weeks at Hartland, staying in a Bed and Breakfast, talking to the fishermen, and getting to know the local history. For shipping it is one of the most dangerous parts of the Devon coast. Attracted by its dizzying scale and cool colouring as well as the changeable weather blown in from the Atlantic, Alan has

Devon – River Otter
Oil on canvas 30 × 24 ins

Sketching at Hartland Quay in North Devon, 1980

Four Silver Jubilee paintings of Hartland commissioned by The University of Exeter to commemorate their Silver Jubilee 1981

been back many times. He has painted well over eighty images of Hartland.

Alan needs these painting forays to keep his ideas fresh. While he was a student at Birmingham College of Art he made his first foreign expedition to Provence, in search of the painting grounds of artists that he admired. 'From the industrial Midlands with all its greyness to arrive in Provence with all the colour – white walls, terracotta roofs, sudden deep shadows, was an incredible experience. I remember going to Cézanne's studio and being astonished at its smallness, how enclosed it was. It was amazing to see all the still life objects he painted still there. It was romantic to see all the places he painted, but still intimidating seeing them through another painter's eyes. What I had to do was move away'. Alan needed to find his own places, unexplored by earlier painters, so that he could see things afresh, 'like a child'. The camping trips to Europe that the Cotton family had taken with their young children had been primarily family holidays, for exploring and sightseeing, although Alan did some drawing where possible, and visited local art galleries. His children still remember spending an entire day in his company in Paris at an exhibition of Soutine's work.

In 1983, for the first time, Alan had the freedom to do some serious painting abroad. At first he took with him masses of materials including huge sheets of pastel paper that were impossibly fragile. He began to develop a method of travelling light, taking only sketchbooks and pens for drawing, and trusting his imagination more when working from these drawings at home. The accumulated drawings, which he never sells, have become an extensive library of ideas from which any number of paintings may be derived. As he says, 'to gain understanding and confidence, drawing for me is always the key. I work from my drawings a lot, even years later. I have spent so much time working on Provence paintings from my drawings that people think of me as a Provence painter.' Alan has found that the atmosphere and immediacy of the drawings remain even when back in the studio, and also that the inevitable time separation between making the drawing and making the painting creates a blurring of edges which allows him to be more imaginative and inventive. He is freer to invent colours, finding that the colour sequences he chooses seem to follow their own special logic when developed intuitively on the palette and on the canvas. A single drawing used in different ways can yield a dozen paintings. 'The process of painting is done not only by mixing the colours on the palette, but also with the aid of the memories evoked by the drawings.'[7] He adds 'Painting is so intuitive. As the work goes on you become more and more imaginative. In a series of paintings most of the better ones are done later. Gradually you get into the spirit of it and you can almost see the images in your mind. Therefore you rely less on the drawing, and more on what comes from inside. You let yourself go totally.'

Hartland – Calm Evening Along the Coast
Oil on canvas 24 x 24 ins

IN PROVENCE Alan searched for painting places that he could make his own. It was the hill towns of the Vaucluse region and especially Gordes that took his breath away. 'Gordes amazed me. I still think it one of the great visual experiences of the world. All the buildings with no foundations cling to a rocky promontory topped by a Renaissance chateau which houses Vasareli's paintings. The way the light plays across the buildings shows up their wonderful geometry. There are all kinds of wonderful curved shapes and little cubes, staccato pinpoints of dark. In the evening you can see the shadow move across the cliff face and the intensity of the light on the topmost buildings increases as the shadow moves up like an intense spotlight. I must have done at least fifty drawings of Gordes, and I always go back there. For a recent exhibition I made a whole lot of new paintings of Gordes. I didn't mean to but I just had to do them.' Alan also discovered the vast ochre quarries of Rustrel and was given a range of ochres from there, which he used in his paintings of the quarries.

Alan explored the hill towns of the Luberon – Bonnieux where Frederick

Gordes, it's amazing

Gore lives, and the beautiful village of Lacoste where he has done a great deal of drawing. He looks for places that give him an intense visual kick, and his engagement with each new painting ground is equally intense. It is not just the visual impact, however, but also the texture of a place and the way people use it, that is important to him. 'For me just to set up an easel anywhere isn't on. I want to know something about the people and the way they live. I like to think that each area that I paint is preceded by an apprenticeship of getting to know the forms, the lights, the moods. Ireland is very different from Provence, with its benign climate and buzzing insects. In Ireland clouds scud in from the Atlantic changing the mood in a moment, and a sombre day can be suddenly washed with light. You imagine people trying to make a living from that land. You paint from imagination finally. No matter how many drawings you do, how many notes you make, you end up working from imagination. Without your personality, your impressions, your reactions, going through the work, it's nothing. Painting is an intellectual as well as a visual and sensual experience.'

Lacoste – Provence
from Place de la Mairie –

Gordes in Golden
Evening Light
Canvas 30 × 24 ins

Alan Cotton

Alan Cotton has lost count of the number of times he has been to Provence. In the early 1980s he went at least twice a year, totally enchanted by the hill towns around Gordes. As he says, 'Provence is all about the good life. It's the most sensuous region to paint. You tend to look at the hill towns on their rocky pinnacles from a distance, but I discovered that by standing on a terrace and looking over the landscape, it gave me a high vantage point, rather like flying, that has always appealed to me. You can look down into the courtyards and see all sorts of wonderful intimate details. There was actually a nude lady in one of the courtyards, and she kept moving as the shadows moved. I find the juxtaposition of the geometric, man-made shapes and the irregular shapes of the land very attractive, and I like to put foreground detail against background space, like making a large scale film that focuses on one or two people set against a big panorama. I have always believed in trying to create spatial depth in a painting and I have used many different devices to create that depth. It's much harder to do it in brilliant light. The diffuse nature of English light makes it easier, but in the sharp light of Provence you have to use different devices, mainly of scale. In this picture the paint used for the foreground is much heavier than that used for the distance.'

Provence – Farmstead and Apple Orchard, Near Gordes, 1988
Oil on canvas 36 x 40 ins

Alan Cotton.
Gordes Aug 1986.

Colin Rowe filming Alan near Gordes in Provence

Provence – Gordes
Oil on canvas 30 × 24 ins

Provence – Golden Valley in the Vaucluse
Oil on canvas 12 x 12 ins

Provence – Sunlit Valley Towards Evening
Oil on canvas 12 x 12 ins

TUSCANY PRESENTED ALAN with new difficulties. Alan went to draw for a month on his own prior to the arrival of a film crew. A BBC film on Alan's work, commissioned by David Pritchard, was later aborted as a result of policy changes scrapping all regional magazine programmes. At this stage, however, the filming was going ahead and Alan was building up a portfolio of drawings and watercolours to be used in it. Drawing in the countryside one day,

troubles in Tuscany

he put his portfolio on the roof of the car and drove away. He was unable to retrieve it, and a month's work was lost. Alan was extremely distressed. In order to replace the necessary work he drew day and night, making himself ill with overwork. Enough new work was completed in time and the film was made, but Alan ended up in hospital with various medical problems, his body having succumbed to the stress. Footage from this filmimg later appeared in the two half hour ITV films *Cotton on Canvas*.

Tuscany – Landscape through the Vines, 1988
Oil on canvas 24 × 30 ins

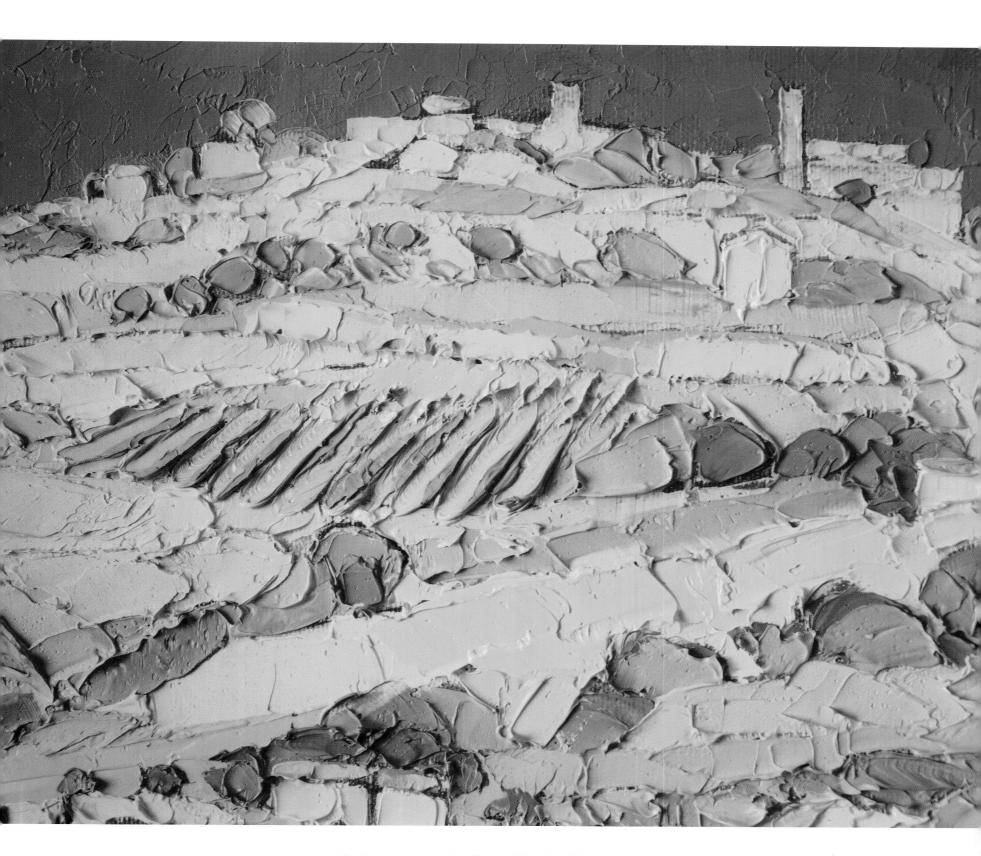

Sunlit Landscape against Stormy Skies, San Gimigniano *(detail)*

FOR SHEER MAGIC OF COLOUR AND FORM Cyprus perhaps took the prize. Alan was persuaded to visit Cyprus by his friend Brian Hoskins, leader of the Red Arrow pilots with whom Alan had flown. When Hoskins was appointed station commander at Akrotiri Alan and Pat went out to see him. Their first visit was a disappointment. It was the wrong time of year and everything was dry and dusty. Hoskins persuaded Alan to return in June, and

fired up by Cyprus

when he did so he found the colours fantastic. 'At the foot of the Troodos mountains where the silt washes down you get these fertile pockets in the valleys where they grow barley and wheat and great thistles about eight feet high. The way the land is divided and plateaux cut from rocks to make fields makes wonderful abstract shapes running through it. I have never been quite so fired up about wanting to paint.'

Cyprus – Summer Landscape, near Paphos, 1992
Oil on canvas 36 x 40 ins

This painting was made after Alan Cotton's second visit to Cyprus in 1990. Exploring Cyprus in June, before the landscape became too dried up, was a revelation. 'Up to that time I had never seen such an amazing range of colour, from pinks and ochres and terracottas right through the spectrum. I was astonished by the starkness of the distance with those arid hills where they try to grow olive trees compared to the fertile silt-laden foreground where you get all those umbelliferous plants shooting through the soil to the height of six feet or more. I have always loved looking at landscape through plants because they reinforce the idea of spatial depth. It is exciting to see something like the head of a thistle close up in great detail and to put it alongside a tiny house seen in the distance. Compared to the more geometric shapes of Provence the landscape of Cyprus is very rhythmical, and the colour more high key. For this painting I washed the canvas with a pale madder brown and worked on it with brown drawing, and I left a lot of the drawing visible. The paint was almost put into a drawn grid, and the marks are more separate and deliberate than usual. It was totally enjoyable finding such a range of marks - from delicate, tiny textured touches with the tip of the knife for seed-heads, to fine linear impressions with the knife's edge for wheat stalks, and then the heavy impasto of a single emphatic stroke for all the solid shapes.

VENICE WAS MORE of a challenge. At first Alan was besieged by memories of countless other painters and their images of the famous old sites. It was not until he began to concentrate on the reflections in the canals that Venice opened up for him like a magic mirror. 'At first I did topographical paintings then began to realise that painting what is familiar is not a good idea. It was only when I took a studio in Venice for the whole summer that I began to work without interference from other paintings I had seen. Some things

in Venice the light changed everything

that you have the greatest desire in the world to paint simply don't come off for you, and you discover that no matter how hard you try you can't hack it. I scrapped my first eight paintings of Venice because I needed to change the way I painted, to use thinner scrapes of paint and softer, more delicate edges. The light changed everything.' Alan explored new ways of putting on the paint and new compositional ideas. The reflected boats and buildings took over most of the canvases, the large areas of painted water becoming a compositional reversal of the wide Irish skies.

Venice – The Old Fish Market, 1995
Oil on canvas 40 x 36 ins

In the early 1980s and 1990s Alan Cotton visited Venice many times, but it was not until he took a studio there for the whole summer that he found his own special places to paint. One of these was the Fish Market, near the Rialto. 'In the Fish Market, just as in a cathedral, you are very aware of the brilliant light outside the building and the very dark interior. The fish are kept fresh by having crushed ice packed around them. The ice melts in the heat and floods the floors, turning them into mirrors that reflect the outside light. People in the market are seen in silhouette against the light. The contrasts of light and dark are extraordinary. Scarlet blinds are used every day to control the light coming in. The light through those red blinds looks very heraldic, a bit like church colours. In this painting the red blinds form the only colour accent against all the cool greys. A farmer with a lovely rotund belly came in and I put him into the picture in stark silhouette. A painting like this has specific dimensions and a human scale that has to be adhered to, but its impact for me was the opportunity to use the drama of light against dark and the reflections on wet surfaces.'

THE COOL COLOURS OF IRELAND were a complete contrast to the brilliant warm colouration of Provence, and Alan's paintings of Ireland demanded new compositional ideas. Where he deliberately omitted the sky from his Provencal paintings, concentrating on the receding shapes and patterns of the land, in Ireland he became increasingly aware of the sky. In his latest series of Irish paintings the horizons have dropped lower and lower and the landmasses have become less important than the skies with their fantastic cloud shapes. The west coast of Ireland fascinates and challenges him. 'In Ireland

a special light

recently I saw this amazing light and I was dancing in and out of the car or charging about on foot, drawing, drawing, getting ideas. I can't leave it alone, chasing the very last of the light.' To find that special light he has been back many times. 'The landscape can be incredibly sombre and it seems almost like the end of the world – the lighting is flat, the rain's coming down, the mist comes down and then suddenly it all moves away and you get great streaks of light across the landscape, like a spotlight illuminating it and there's all the magic – the magic of colour, the magic of form.' [8]

Connemara – Early Morning Along the Bay, 1988
Oil on canvas 24 x 32 ins

Alan is drawn to the west coast of Ireland, and has explored it on many occasions. The toughness of the landscape contrasts with the softness of the countryside around his home in Devon, and he relishes the difficulties of depicting it. 'The weather is more unpredictable than anywhere I know. On the occasion that gave birth to this painting we were staying at the Renvyle Hotel and we had had three days of drizzle, with misty conditions that made it not very inspiring to paint. I was debating whether to stay on or to come home. I woke at 5 am and looked out of the hotel window and there was this magical dawn coming up, with the light breaking through great clouds. I was filled with excitement to see some light at last , but also to see this amazing piece of theatre. I quickly dressed and rushed out on my own and scribbled notes and bits of drawing, much of it pretty rough as it was done on the hoof. I made a whole series of paintings from those three hours of drawing. That dawn was one of those moments when you are filled with such a passionate excitement that you want to hold on to it, to own it. Back in the studio you have to remember that initial excitement.'

THE PIEMONTE REGION in the north of Italy is another area which Alan has made particularly his own. Having known Mario Gerlotto, a local Devon restaurateur, for several years, he grew tired of hearing him say how wonderful his native countryside was. One day he said, 'Ok, let's go'. Mario took him into the heart of his own world, into the circle of his family and friends. Through Mario Alan got to know the culture and way of life of a little explored area of Italy. Mario introduced Alan to everybody as the important painter whose pictures of their countryside would be exhibited in London, and Alan was treated with enormous generosity. As Alan drew among the vineyards,

deep shadows between the rows. I had been alerted by Mario that the late autumn was the time to come, but it was still a seminal moment for me to see those unbelievable colours. The landscape rolls and rolls and you get deep crimson, scarlet, purple in the foreground and swashes of colour as you move through the landscape. It was a new colour experience to be close up against huge vines with the light coming through them, making translucent jewels of colour. Between the vine leaves the pale blue-grey mists can be seen.'

With Mario's help Alan arranged a painting course in his village of Serravalle Langhe. The generosity of the villagers made this course special. As the twenty

Piemonte, he made it his own

Mario, like an excited schoolboy, would drop grapes into his mouth or bring him pomegranates, cherries and nuts to eat. He found little hostelries with delicious food on offer. Gradually the imagery of Piemonte started to fill Alan's mind, and he has been back many times at different times of the year. "I've never seen so many images in one square mile. In Piemonte you don't have to work hard to find motifs. The terrain is so hilly and the weather changes amazingly so that you get mists in the valleys. Churches and chateaux are built on the high points and there's a mystery everywhere. The landscape is patterned by the vines, which cast

students entered Serravalle Langhe the church bells rang out and all the inhabitants came into the village square to greet them. A welcoming feast was laid out for them and a concert was staged in a twelfth century chapel, with ancient frescoes on the wall, which also served as the studio for the week. During the week, as Alan and the course tutor Ray Balkwill did the rounds of their students, they would find easels abandoned while the students were invited in to share meals with the family nearby.

Mario Gerlotto (left) and Alan enjoy a glass of wine with friends in the vineyard

Piemonte – Patterns of the Vines
Oil on canvas 36 × 36 ins

Piemonte – Alan watches as Cesare's dog finds the rare white truffle *(above)*

Alan drawing in a Piemonte vineyard, November 1999 *(below)*

David, Mario and Alan talk to the children at a playgroup in Serravalle Langhe *(top right)*

Discussing Alan's drawing book *(middle)*

Alan and Mario enjoy lunch *al fresco* with the Devon Painters in Piemonte *(bottom right)*

Piemonte – Rhythms of the Vines
Oil on canvas 36 × 36 ins.

ALAN'S EAGERNESS to share his enthusiasm for certain landscapes with students has not always been so spectacularly well rewarded. His passion for Provence induced him, in true buccaneering spirit, to take up a suggestion through a friend of a friend to run a painting course at a new 'International Arts Centre' in Fayence. Trusting that all the facilities would be exactly as glowingly described, Alan invited his brother Bernard and family to join the group, and both families drove down through France with their cars filled with the equipment for the course. Alan's car had reached Montelimar when his engine blew up. Bernard, furious with his brother for creating major problems, nevertheless agreed to take on all the equipment while Alan and family proceeded by train to Nice. Arriving very late at Nice station, they saw Bernard drive up with his car still fully loaded, having been unable to find the International Arts Centre. The owner, a Madame Nonnay who had promised to meet them, was nowhere to be found. After a night in the railway hotel Alan and Bernard set off in search of the centre. After an abortive morning they finally found an hotelier who knew of

sharing has its problems

her whereabouts. 'Don't have anything to do with her – she is mad!' In desperation, with visions of the students about to arrive haunting them, they drove to the place he suggested. It was a surreal experience. They had to leave the car and walk across fields full of shoulder-high grass, passing a three-legged dog and a monkey tethered to a tree. The promised studio facilities consisted of a filthy building full of broken furniture draped in an enormous Union Jack. Part of the living accommodation was inhabited by a colony of hippies. How could they deal with such an appalling situation? Both families set to and laboured to the point of exhaustion to get the studio into some sort of working order, and to find alternative accommodation for some of the imminently arriving students. The hippies were persuaded to move out, and in a combined attempt to get rid of old mattresses crawling with lice they inadvertently set fire to the campus, bringing out the fire brigade and the police. The students arrived and the course went ahead. By keeping everyone tipsy all week with wine flowing freely, Alan survived. His problems, however, were not over. His car was defunct and he had to get his family and all his equipment back to England. As Bernard agreed to take both families home, Alan's penance was to transport all the luggage. He loaded it all into his daughter's pram and with this precarious edifice he caught the train to Paris. In Paris late at night he changed stations, pushing the loaded pram before him like a refugee. One of its wheels collapsed and its contents fell out on the station escalator. Exhausted, Alan checked in to the nearest hotel which could offer him only the honeymoon suite. He spent a solitary night soaking in a palatial bath and trying to sleep on a vast coin-operated bed that gyrated through every axis.

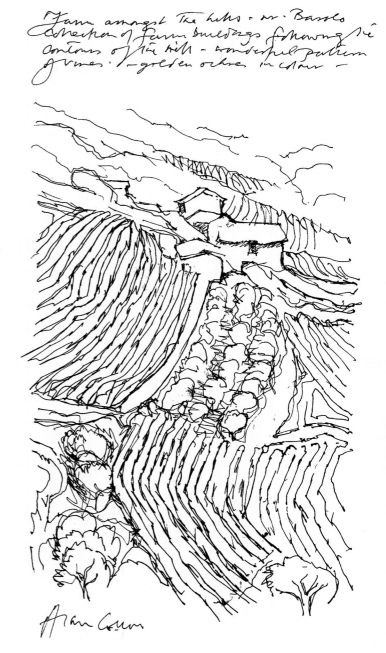

Piemonte – Evening Vines
Oil on canvas 20 x 20 ins

I N THE COTTON FAMILY the ethos is that 'you don't just take, you give'. Alan is very aware of living within a community and it is important to him to share his enthusiasms. Although he feels immensely privileged to be able to spend his life painting and to sell his work so well, he is no ivory tower painter. 'I like ordinary people and I want my work to be accessible to ordinary people. I can't bear pretentious art – I find it embarrassing.' [9] He likes to help other struggling painters and is an energetic participant in many art-related activities, lecturing, making films, and organising exhibitions. In 2000 he was instrumental in founding the South West Academy of Fine and Applied Arts, based in Exeter, becoming its first President. With a group of friends and colleagues – Graham and Annie Ovenden, Michael Morgan, Gentian Sims and others – Alan has worked hard to get its programme of exhibitions going, and to maintain a high quality both in the work displayed and in the catalogues that

Left to right: Bill Holland, Alan and Lizzie Holland in the garden at Brockhill Studio, 1998

you don't just take, you give

accompany each exhibition. The South West Academy has been an immense success, providing Exeter with the first real focus for practising artists. Its value to the area is incalculable.

Throughout his life his relationships both with family and friends have been of the utmost importance to Alan. He has always been very much a family man, a 'hands on' father whose approachability and problem-solving capacity is deeply appreciated by his children. His close friendships with his children have enriched his life and continue to do so. His friendships with other people encountered during his career have been equally valuable. Kevin Crooks, whom he met through filming, was until his death in 2001 Alan's closest friend for over twenty years. He also values the friendship of many other artists, including the sculptor Denis Mitchell and the painters Terry Frost, John Miller and Ken Howard. Jim Watson of the Canada Arts Gallery was an important ally. Bill Holland, the head of Universal Classics and Jazz, whose daughter wrote an A level thesis on Alan's painting, has been a seminal influence in opening up the world of music for him. David Messum not only has Alan's interests at heart but shares his love of fast cars. Brian Hoskins, an avid collector of Alan's work, has taken him flying and shares his love of speed. Martin Bralsford, a collector whom Alan met at one of his Private Views in Jersey, has played an important part in his life. He now owns a large collection of Alan's paintings and has invited him to design sets for an opera to be staged at the Jersey Opera House. The actor Art Malik, whom Alan met at David Messum's Lordswood Private View, has become a great friend, and it was he who inspired Alan to go to Morocco in search of new painting material. Sean Cluskey of the renowned Doyle's Sea Food Restaurant in Dingle, introduced Alan to the magnificent Blasket Islands. Alan stays with Sean on his frequent visits to Co. Kerry.

Kevin Crooks with Alan in the studio

Actor Dudley Sutton, painter Rose Hilton and Alan in Cornwall

With Dennis Mitchell and John Wells outside their studio in Newlyn, 1985

During a break in filming at Kitley Manor for Carlton TV. Left to Right: Annie Ovenden, Alan Cotton, Ken Howard, John Miller and Graham Ovenden

Alan and Pat Cotton, David Messum and Carol Tee in the studio *(above)*

Hugh Scully, Kevin Crooks and Alan at the Private View of *An Artist Abroad* at the David Messum Gallery in London, 1990 *(below)*

Alan and Sir Peter Blake at the Private View of the first South West Academy Open Exhibition, 2000 *(top right)*

Jimmy Gardner the actor with Alan at a Private View *(middle)*

David Messum, Alan Cotton and John Miller at Alan's first night preview at the David Messum Gallery in London, 1989 *(bottom right)*

Evening Light at Harvest Time in Provence
Oil on canvas 24 x 30 ins

Michael Morgan, formerly head of the Froebel Institute and a painter/collaborator in founding the South West Academy, has become a close friend and confidant. No less important is the friendship of the painters Graham and Annie Ovenden. There are many others whose companionship enriches Alan's life and gives him enormous pleasure.

Alan is a sociable character, and in his relationships gives as much as he receives. He believes in playing an active part in the community in which he lives. However, the vital element in Alan's life is painting. It is through his celebratory paintings that he shares his enthusiasms. Looking at landscape fills him with joy. In his paintings he tries to create a parallel landscape that will give the viewer a similar joy. His work is essentially optimistic and celebratory, and he admits 'I'm a romantic about life despite all the evidence to the contrary'. His love of paint and the whole process of painting is as strong as his love of landscape. 'Painting is like being a child again, playing with simple ingredients to create light and shade, warmth and coolness, softness and

all my paintings are made from drawings

hardness. You are trying to set up a series of shapes and rhythms which represent your experience.'

During the last twenty years Alan has established a working practice that suits him well. Out on location, in the countryside, he draws. 'I think drawing, unlike painting, is a craft. Now I draw as a natural process, with an easy facility like handwriting. At art school I was never told that the purpose of drawing is a thinking process, to enable one to select, to construct, to eliminate, to go right for the jugular. The immediacy of drawing is that you are part of a bigger environment. You feel the sun on your back, the wind in your hair, the smells around you. This is all part of what goes into you to produce the painting. There's no short cut for it. Occasionally I use a photograph as an aide-memoire if I'm on the move, but essentially all my paintings are made from drawings. A studio is a very cloistered environment. You can control all the elements – the light, the music, the amount of coffee you have. Outdoors is much more chancy.'

Now at the height of his powers as a painter, Alan Cotton holds a position deep at the heart of English landscape painting. He is one of the long line of British painters, from J W M Turner and Samuel Palmer to John Piper and Alan Reynolds, whose belief in nature as a subject worth interpreting and celebrating in paint has remained unshaken. It is a romantic vision based on the implicit notion that the beauty of the countryside, when reinterpreted in painting, has a kind of redemptive power. Also implicit in this vision is the idea that art itself is redemptive, that it conveys an optimism, a message of hope. This is the conclusion to which John Berger came in his musings on art, and it is this essential optimism that underlies all Alan's painting.

Now that Art embraces such a wide variety of different methods and mediums, oil painting on canvas is seen as part of an old tradition, and any painter in oils is necessarily a traditionalist. Alan is proud to be such a traditionalist. Never mind the abundance of assemblage, conceptual and performance work, paint remains the best way of purveying colour, and colour is what his paintings are about. Colour has not been superceded as a major protagonist in conveying mood and emotion, and it is the mood of a scene, tranquil, mysterious, or joyful, that he seeks to convey. He constructs his images in the classical way, aiming for harmony. His colour combinations also seek harmony, or rather a harmonious settling of contradictions. It is in his application of paint that he diverges from classical tradition. The thick, juicy impasto of his oil paint is distinctly twentieth century, and owes much to the creative examples of Chaim Soutine and Kyffin Williams. In Alan's work the paint itself, and not simply the colour it purveys, becomes an important factor in what is effectively an image in low relief, creating a surface texture with its own special dynamics.

Back at home in the studio amidst stacks of paint and a huge array of painting knives, he works on the images. 'Although painting is solitary, I don't think it is necessarily lonely. The good days are when it goes well and you're uninterrupted. I'm very much a morning painter, and increasingly getting earlier and earlier. I can work from 6 am. I like to put in a long spurt of time, until say 1 pm. That's solid work. Then I need to be outside. The psychological space is as important as the physical space, and I try to spend some time by the sea. I might walk by the sea and then come back and work from 5 to 7 pm or so. I can't work later than that. I'm paranoid about getting into the studio in the morning, and feel bad if I don't put in the hours. It's to do with my background and a strong work ethic.'

'With all the painting I've done I can still make a false start. Any good painter does bad paintings, because you're always trying something out. You can go up many a gum tree. If you work only within the craft you have learnt your work will go downhill and look second-hand. A sense of discovery is important. Sometimes you can take a drawing and move so far from the original that it becomes a new phenomenon. The buzz of adventure is necessary. Some paintings are a great pleasure to do, others are a struggle. Occasionally I have had marvellous times in my studio when I have surprised myself. I couldn't wait to get the next mark on in case the whole thing evaporated. There are times when you work in a timeless zone. You are on to something and the excitement is such that you don't want to let it go.'

The paintings that pour out of Alan Cotton's studio are hard won. They are the result of a long process of looking and drawing, thinking and laying down the paint, scraping back and reconsidering. The pictorial space is explored, suggested, defined, with every variety of mark at Alan's disposal. The variety of subject matter forces him to invent new marks. But it is a romance with the landscape that underlies all his painting. All of his work is infused with the love of being alive in a beautiful world.

Alan with Sir Terry Frost *(left)*

During the filming of 'Cotton on Canvas' with Hugh Scully *(below)*

Flight preparations with Brian Hoskins of the Red Arrows *(above)*

At home with Art Malik *(below)*

Alan and Sean Cluskey on Great Blasket Island, Co. Kerry *(below left)*

Devon

Alan Cotton's move from the Forest of Dean to Devon provided him with a range of completely new subjects for his paintings. The great skyscapes of St Briavel's Common had drawn his eye upwards and outwards. Around the River Otter in Devon he found himself looking downwards into gently folded valleys, into the detail of bank and hedgerow, down into the reflections on pond and river water. The morning sparkle of the river and its satiny sheen on a calm evening inspired a series of lyrical paintings in which he explored the changing patterns created by the fall of light and shade on the water and on the surrounding vegetation.

Hartland, on Devon's north coast, offered a bracing contrast to the lush farmland and river valleys of South Devon. Alan's response to the dramatic sight of the great sea mass constantly hitting the slabs of rock and cliff was vivid and immediate. It was a painter's response to an external scene that seemed to match his own internal painting world. He was so overwhelmed by it that he wanted to hold on to it, to make it his own, to paint a whole series of pictures. He returned to Hartland many times, getting to know the history of the place, drawing it at different times of day, in all seasons and all weathers. As a painting ground Hartland symbolised adventure - the adventure of experimenting with new ways of painting to describe it adequately. The scale had to be large - larger than he had previously worked on - and the palette restricted. Every painting explored the relationship between the static land and the moving mass of water. The application of the paint had to be as energetic as the movement of water, and Alan found that the dynamic of the painting knife helped. He used all his muscle power to attack the big canvases with a fully charged painting knife.

Beside the River Otter

GLYN LOMAX

Hartland Morning
Oil on canvas 40 x 60 ins

Otter Valley Morning
Oil on canvas 14 × 20 ins

Barley Heads
Oil on canvas 20 × 16 ins

Blackberry Hedgerow
Oil on canvas 18 × 24 ins

The Hidden Valley
Oil on canvas 24 × 30 ins

Provence

As a student - and later with his family - Alan Cotton had made pilgrimages to Provence to see the painting grounds of artists such as Cézanne for himself. It was not until he resigned from teaching, however, that he began to explore the South of France as a subject for his own painting. During the 1980s he travelled to Provence two or three times a year, returning home with hundreds of drawings from which to work. He was thrilled by the hill towns of Provence, especially Gordes, with its juxtaposition of geometric man-made shapes and irregular landscape shapes, and by the way the light hit the buildings, making dark staccato pinpricks. Watching the shadow climbing the cliff face and the light intensifying until the topmost buildings seemed spot-lit gave him intense visual pleasure. He also loved the way the orchards strode across the rolling landmasses, casting diminishing patterns of shade. Provence presented Alan with a landscape shaped and patterned by generations of mankind, planned and cultivated under a southern sun and proclaiming from every corner 'this is the good life'. Alan began to seek out high vantage points, rather like flying, to look over

Working at Gordes

With Colin Rowe (cameraman), Zyna Gaskell-Brown (sound) and Philip Speight (director) during the filming in Provence of *Cotton on Canvas*

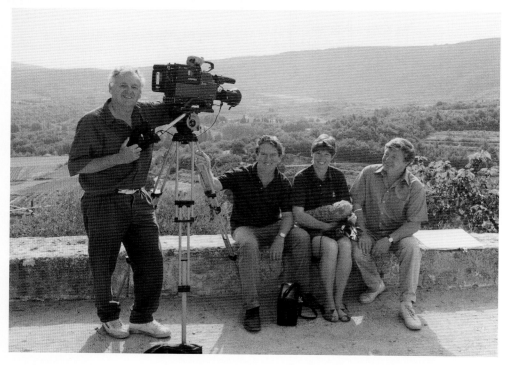

the land, and his paintings concentrated on describing the vast panoramas below, often dispensing with any visible sky. His desire to create great spatial depth gave him new insights into the relationship between foreground and distance. It was like making a big-scale film with the focus on people in a foreground set against huge expanses of scenery. He experimented with many ways of creating spatial depth - varying the scale, creating linear or staccato progressions across and into the picture, and using a heavier paint impasto in the foreground. The brilliant light of Provence, where colours are not diffused by distance as in softer English light, made spatial depth harder to achieve, but brought him a new understanding of tonal contrast and a new range of colours to his palette.

Sunlight and Shadow Near Fayence
Oil on canvas 20 x 20 ins

Orchards near Gordes – Almond Blossom
Oil on canvas   20 x 16 ins

Almond Blossom at Gordes
Oil on canvas 24 x 30 ins

Late Summer Landscape – Building the Hayricks
Oil on canvas   24 x 30 ins

Buying the Bread – Early Morning in Bonnieux *(opposite)*
Oil on canvas   40 x 36 ins

Sunlight and Shadow on the Luberon Plain
Oil on canvas 18 x 24 ins

Gordes in Early Evening Light
Oil on canvas 24 x 30 ins

Farm in Red Landscape, near Roussillon
Oil on canvas 20 × 24 ins

Gordes – Provence
Oil on canvas 30 × 24 ins

Vines near Arles
Oil on canvas   20 x 16 ins

Apple Orchards and Irises at Bonnieux
Oil on canvas   24 x 30 ins

A Lane in Gordes
Oil on canvas 10 x 12 ins

Vista Across the Luberon – Bonnieux
Oil on canvas 20 x 16 ins

Apple Orchard and Distant Views to Bonnieux
Oil on canvas 16 x 14 ins

Provence – Lavender Fields in the Luberon
Oil on canvas 12 x 12 ins

Provence – The Luberon Plain
Oil on canvas 10 x 12 ins

The Road to Gordes
Oil on canvas 12 x 10 ins

Provence – Farm Amongst the Hills
Oil on canvas 12 x 12 ins

The Road to Bonnieux – Evening Light
Oil on canvas   30 × 60 ins

Red Evening Landscape at Roussillon
Oil on canvas 24 × 30 ins

The Ochre Quarry at Rustrel *(opposite)*
Oil on canvas 36 × 40 ins

Cyprus

Alan's first visit to Cyprus was at the invitation of Brian Hoskins, the Red Arrows pilot and his wife Lizzie, when Brian was Station Commander at RAF Akrotiri. That initial visit was a disappointment to Alan as it proved to be a time of year when everything was dry and dusty and a flat light bleached out all the colours. It was not until his second visit in June 1990 that Alan saw for the first time the great range of colours in the landscape, from pinks and ochres to terracottas and purples. He was astonished by the contrast of the arid hills dotted with olive trees and the fertile silty valleys full of immensely tall plants. Since childhood he had loved looking at landscape through plants, and Cyprus gave him many opportunities to paint the detail of plants close-up against distant fields and hills. The abstract shapes created by the way the land was divided, with plateaux cut from the rocks to make fields, excited him. In Cyprus he found a more rhythmical landscape than the geometric shapes of Provence, and a higher colour key. He was so fired up with images from Cyprus that on his return home he swiftly made eighteen very large paintings. These pictures flowed. They seemed almost to paint themselves, and Alan experienced the magical feeling of working in a timeless zone.

Cyprus – Crops and Olive Trees, Evening Light
Oil on canvas 24 × 30 ins

Harvest and Summer Foliage near Paphos
Oil on canvas 26 × 30 ins

Summer Landscape near Paphos *(opposite)*
Oil on canvas 36 × 40 ins

Plants against a Hillside
Oil on canvas 20 × 16 ins

Vines and Olive Trees
Oil on canvas   24 x 30 ins

Landscape Across a Wheatfield
Oil on canvas 10 x 12 ins

Plants Against a Hillside II
Oil on canvas 24 × 20 ins

Harvest Landscape in Cyprus
Pastel 10 x 14 ins

Landscape near Paphos with Wheatfields and Foreground Plants
Oil on canvas 24 × 30 ins

Summer Landscape near Paphos
Oil on canvas 24 x 20 ins

Landscape near Paphos *(opposite)*
Oil on canvas 36 x 40 ins

Tuscany

Alan had always wanted to paint in Tuscany, and in the late 1980s he rented for several months a house in the small village of Strove. The village church was completely surrounded by a farmyard and Alan often found himself drawing among the hens. He found it difficult to paint in well-known places such as San Gimigniano, and it took him a while to find his own subjects. The loss of a quantity of drawings and the sudden onset of illness explains, perhaps, why he has not up to now returned to this particular painting ground. A fine series of landscapes, however, seen through repoussoirs of vineyards and orchards, resulted from this single visit.

Working at Strove, Tuscany, 1989

Sunlit Landscape Against Stormy Skies
Oil on canvas 24 x 30 ins

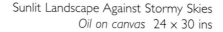

Vineyards near San Gimigniano
Oil on canvas 16 x 20 ins

Vines in a Wheatfield at Strove, Evening Light
Oil on canvas 16 x 20 ins

Tuscany – Sunlight after the Storm
Oil on canvas 10 x 12 ins

Tuscany – Church and Orchard
Oil on canvas 36 x 40 ins

Piemonte

Alan was persuaded to visit Piemonte by his friend Mario Gerlotto. With Mario Alan explored Piemonte's rolling countryside, seeing painting motifs wherever he went. The hilly terrain, with its chateaux and churches built on the high points, and the changeable weather, with mists hanging in the valleys, created an enticing air of mystery. In late autumn the crimsons, scarlets, and deep purples of the vines with the light shining through them appeared almost fluorescent, and, contrasted with the pale blue-grey mists, were a new colour experience. Images of Piemonte soon started to take him over. Alan has returned many times at different times of year, when the grapes for the famous Barolo wine are picked or when the rare white truffles are unearthed. His Piemonte paintings range in scale from details of vine leaves against mist to broad panoramas of rolling terraced farmland topped by distant villages, and in colour from subdued ochres and greens to the most brilliant carmines and burnt oranges.

In the Vineyards, Piemonte, with Mario and David

Castello della Volta. Piemonte Italy. Alan Cotton

Rows of Vines at Montelupo Albese
Oil on canvas 36 x 36 ins

Autumn in Diano d'Alba
Oil on canvas 24 x 24 ins

Early Morning Light in the Langhe
Oil on canvas 20 x 20 ins

Cottages Amongst the Vines
Oil on canvas 12 x 12 ins

Montelupo Albese in Evening Light
Oil on canvas 24 x 24 ins

Venice

In Venice Alan soon realised that painting very familiar scenes was not a good idea. It was only when he took a studio in Venice that he began to paint without interference from other paintings that he had seen. He found his own particular motifs in places where the scene was transfigured by light on water. The reflections on rain-washed piazzas, or on the fishmarket's great mirror-like floor, awash with melted ice, provided the impetus for many paintings. But above all it was the reflections in the small canals that fascinated him. The way the light hit the facades of the buildings and was reflected in water which then assumed most unwatery colours, made a powerful impact. His colours became hot and high-key, echoing the red and yellow hues of the painted buildings reflected in narrow canals where little sky light leaks through. Compositionally Alan was breaking new ground with vertical paintings composed almost entirely of reflections, striped with the

elongated mirror images of buildings and poles, and hung from a narrow top margin of solid objects - boats, gondolas, the bases of buildings - used as reference points. The thick paint, freely applied with the knife, parallelled the viscous quality of the water in these small, still canals.

Venice – Reflections along the Fondamenta Dei Mori
Oil on canvas 20 x 20 ins

Vertical Reflections in Calm
Waters
Oil on canvas 24 x 24 ins

Jagged Reflections in Sunlight
and Shadow *(opposite)*
Oil on canvas   24 x 20 ins

Canal Reflections in
Accademia
Oil on canvas 30 x 24 ins

Canal Reflections in
Early Morning Light
Oil on canvas
30 x 24 ins

The End of the Storm
Oil on canvas 12 × 10 ins

The Old Fish Market
Pastel   24 x 18 ins

Evening Light on the Grand Canal
Oil on canvas 20 x 16 ins

The Narrow Canal
Oil on canvas
30 × 24 ins

Ireland

Going to Connemara to find a change of artistic diet after years of painting in Mediterranean lands, Alan encountered days of drizzle and little visibility. Debating whether to abandon the attempt and go home, he chanced to see a magical dawn, where pale yellow light broke in long rays through great livid clouds. This piece of natural theatre was a turning point, encouraging him to go back many times in different seasons and weathers. He found Ireland's weather the most unpredictable he had ever experienced. The light effects were awe-inspiring, and for Alan the challenge was to note down these fleeting effects vividly enough so that his initial excitement could be instantly recalled when painting back in the studio. Many of Alan's drawings, made 'on the hoof', were rapid sketches speckled and blotched with rain that accentuated the sense of urgency and movement that would find its way into paintings made at home. He used a restricted palette of blues and ochres, the Irish light inviting strongly tonal compositions with low horizons and wide skies. The rugged romanticism of Ireland's west coast drew Alan back again and again, and he was fascinated by the way succeeding generations have endeavoured to scratch a living in the harshest of conditions. With undiminished enthusiasm he has explored Connemara and Galway, Donegal and County Kerry, the Dingle Peninsula and the Blasket Isles.

Donegal – The Coast Road to Kilcar
Oil on canvas   36 x 36 ins

Connemara – Spring Landscape
Oil on canvas   20 x 20 ins

Co. Kerry – Dingle Bay at Sunset
Oil on canvas   24 x 24 ins

Connemara – A Cluster of Cottages, Ballyconneely
Oil on canvas 16 x 20 ins

Co. Kerry – Cottages at Ventry Harbour
Oil on canvas 30 x 36 ins

Connemara – Reflections on Wet Sand
Oil on canvas 14 x 14 ins

Connemara – The Last of the Storm
Oil on canvas 24 x 24 ins

Co. Kerry – Farm near the Village of Ardamore
Oil on canvas 30 x 36 ins

Co. Kerry – Bay along the Dingle Peninsula
Oil on canvas 36 x 40 ins

Morocco

For Alan Cotton, part of the excitement of visiting a new place is that it forces him to think, and perhaps to paint, in a new way. It was his friend, the actor Art Malik, who persuaded Alan to go to Morocco for the first time in January 2002. He went to Marrakech and the Atlas Mountains where he was amazed by the scale of the landscape and its unusual shapes and colour combinations. The light, too, was extraordinary, illuminating long sequences of earth colours, from umber and sienna to pale Naples yellow, and creating an infinite variety of lilacs and purples in the shadows. Finding that he could not recreate the luminosity of these brilliant evening-lit colours with a thick impasto, Alan experimented with thin coloured glazes and with scraping and staining his canvases. Morocco is another painting ground that has led him to develop new compositional ideas and new ways of applying the paint. These striated, flowing landscapes have a strength and vibrancy which stems from this fresh approach.

Getting to know the locals – Alan and David

In the Souk at Marrakech
Oil on canvas 20 x 20 ins

Jemaa el Fna at Midday – Marrakech
Oil on canvas   20 x 20 ins

Goats in the High Atlas
Oil on canvas 24 x 24 ins

Acknowledgements

Working on this book has been a most enjoyable experience. My thanks go to Alan and Pat Cotton for their invaluable encouragement and advice as well as their generous, patient hospitality through days and days of talking and looking at paintings. My thanks go also to David Messum and Carol Tee of Messum's Fine Art for their unstinting support, and for their flair and professionalism in designing this handsome book. Many a glass of wine has sealed a harmonious working relationship between the five of us.

Writing the biography of a living artist is quite different from most art history. It is as much about the human condition as about the art, and what emerges are the psychological motivations and deciding factors that turn a human being into an artist. This life story, based on direct evidence, has, I hope, the freshness of a living record.

Jenny Pery
April 2003

Fine art photography by John Saunders

Footnotes

All the quotations in this book are from recorded conversations between Alan Cotton and Jenny Pery held in November and December 2001, unless otherwise indicated below.

1 Living France, February 2001, issue 106

2 France, Autumn 1993, article by Alan Cotton

3 David Messum Fine Art, Alan Cotton exhibition catalogue 1988

4 Emma Burn, unpublished manuscript

5 Emma Burn, unpublished manuscript

6 Graham Hughes, Arts Review, 23 September 1988

7 David Messum Fine Art, Alan Cotton exhibition catalogue 1988

8 Devon Life, April 2001, article by Alan Cotton

9 Emma Burn, unpublished manuscript